A LITTLE EARLY LEARNING POEM BOOK ABOUT THE LETTER F

A Little Early Learning Poem Book about the Letter F

Walter the Educator

Silent King Books

SILENT KING BOOKS

SKB

Copyright © 2024 by Walter the Educator

All rights reserved. No part of this book may be reproduced in any manner whatsoever without written permission except in the case of brief quotations embodied in critical articles and reviews.

First Printing, 2024

Disclaimer
This book is a literary work; poems are not about specific persons, locations, situations, and/or circumstances unless mentioned in a historical context. This book is for entertainment and informational purposes only. The author and publisher offer this information without warranties expressed or implied. No matter the grounds, neither the author nor the publisher will be accountable for any losses, injuries, or other damages caused by the reader's use of this book. The use of this book acknowledges an understanding and acceptance of this disclaimer.

dedicated to all the early learners
across the world

THE LETTER F

In fields of fanciful flowers, far from fretful foes,

Frolicking foxes frolic, as the gentle zephyr blows.

Fickle fairies flit and flutter, with their wings so fine,

Fostering friendships, forging fun, beneath the sunshine's shine.

Furry friends frolic freely, in forests lush and green,

Frogs frolic in the foliage, with their croaks unseen.

Fables whispered by the fireside, fueling youthful dreams,

Fascinating flocks of feathered friends, in flight, they gleam.

Families frolic on the shore, by foamy waves of sea,

Feasting on fish, fresh and fine, in flavors fancy-free.

Frisky felines frolic, with their fur so soft and sleek,

Fawns frolic in the fields, as the sun begins to peak.

Fancy dress-up, fairy tales, and funny-faced clowns,

Festive feasts of fruit and fudge, and fizzy drinks that drown.

Ferris wheels and flying kites, in the wide and open air,

Fireworks flashing, fizzling out, leaving trails so rare.

Folklore from forgotten times, where knights in armor fought,

Fierce dragons flying high, in fiery battles sought.

Fumbling fingers finding fun, in fabrications fine,

Fabled kingdoms far away, where fantasies entwine.

Frosted cookies, fluffy cakes, and flavors that delight,

Fizzy drinks and fruity treats, fill the festive night.

Fragrant flowers, freshly picked, in fields of faded blue,

Frosty mornings, frozen ponds, where frosty fairies flew.

Fickle fortune favors those who fearlessly pursue,

Fervent dreams and fantasies, where the future's hue.

Flaming fires flicker, fade, in the fading light of day,

Fledgling hopes and faltering fears, they falter and they sway.

Festive frolics, fabled tales, and frothy mugs of cheer,

Flickering flames and fleeting dreams, that slowly disappear.

Forgotten whispers, fading fast, in the fabric of the night,

Fleeting moments, flying by, in the fading twilight.

Faint echoes of forgotten times, in the far-off distant past,

Fragile flowers, fading fast, in the fierce and bitter blast.

Fading footsteps, falling leaves, in the forest's fleeting grace,

Fleeting fantasies and fickle dreams, in the flickering fireplace.

Fearless knights and fiery dragons, in the forest deep,

Flickering torches, fading fast, in the night's embrace.

Fragile hearts and fleeting hopes, in the fading light,

Fleeting dreams and fickle fears, in the fabric of the night.

Frosty mornings, frozen ponds, where frosty fairies flew,

Flickering flames and fading dreams, in the fading light of day.

Fragile flowers, fading fast, in the fierce and bitter blast,

Faint echoes of forgotten times, in the far-off distant past.

Fickle fortune favors those who fearlessly pursue,

Fervent dreams and fantasies, where the future's hue.

Fabled tales and fickle dreams, in the flickering fireplace,

Fleeting moments, flying by, in the fading twilight's grace.

ABOUT THE CREATOR

Walter the Educator is one of the pseudonyms for Walter Anderson. Formally educated in Chemistry, Business, and Education, he is an educator, an author, a diverse entrepreneur, and he is the son of a disabled war veteran. "Walter the Educator" shares his time between educating and creating. He holds interests and owns several creative projects that entertain, enlighten, enhance, and educate, hoping to inspire and motivate you.

Follow, find new works, and stay up to date with Walter the Educator™ at WaltertheEducator.com

www.ingramcontent.com/pod-product-compliance
Lightning Source LLC
LaVergne TN
LVHW010618070526
838199LV00063BA/5188